The Emancipation Proclamation

Why Lincoln Really Freed the Slaves

The Emancipation Proclamation

Why Lincoln Really Freed the Slaves

★ ★ ★

BY ROBERT YOUNG, 1951-

WITHDRAWN

 **DILLON PRESS**
New York

Maxwell Macmillan Canada
Toronto

Maxwell Macmillan International
New York Oxford Singapore Sydney

For Ray,
who always has the right book

Acknowledgments

The author would like to thank Clarence G. Seckel, Jr., for his generous assistance.

Photo Credits

Photo research by Debbie Needleman
Cover courtesy of the Surratt House and Tavern
Surratt House and Tavern: title page, 6; Lincoln Art Publishing Company: 11; Massachusetts Commandery Military Order of the Loyal Legion and the U.S. Army Military History Institute: 12, 13, 31, 55; Schomburg Center for Research in Black Culture: 20, 29, 34, 43 (top), 62; The Boston Athenaeum: 24, 25, 35, 36, 37 (bottom), 39, 58; Massachusetts Historical Society: 37 (top); Virginia Historical Society: 43 (bottom), 45, 51; Anne S. K. Brown Military Collection, Brown University: 56; Debbie Needleman: 64.

Book Design by Carol Matsuyama

Library of Congress Cataloging-in-Publication Data

Young, Robert, 1951–
   The Emancipation Proclamation : why Lincoln really freed the slaves / by Robert Young.
      p. cm. — (Both sides)
   Includes bibliographical references and index.
   ISBN 0-87518-613-0
   1. Slaves—United States—Emancipation—Juvenile literature. 2. Afro-Americans—History—1863–1877—Juvenile literature. 3. United States. Presidents (1861–1865 : Lincoln). Emancipation Proclamation—Juvenile literature. I. Title. II. Series: Both sides (Dillon Press)
   E453.Y68 1994   94-9361
   973.7'14—dc20

A debate concerning the several reasons that prompted President Lincoln to issue the Emancipation Proclamation

Dillon Press
Macmillan Publishing Company
866 Third Avenue
New York, NY 10022

Maxwell Macmillan Canada, Inc.
1200 Eglinton Avenue East
Suite 200
Don Mills, Ontario M3C 3N1

Macmillan Publishing Company is part of the Maxwell Communication Group of Companies.

First edition

Printed in the United States of America

10 9 8 7 6 5 4 3 2 1

0-382-24712-4 (pbk.)

★ ★ ★ **Contents** ★ ★ ★

In this old sketch, a somber note pervades the atmosphere as
Lincoln signs the fateful document freeing the slaves.

ONE

January 1, 1863

Thursday, January 1, 1863, was a bright, crisp day in Washington, D.C. President Abraham Lincoln awoke early. He had a busy day ahead of him. There was paperwork to do and meetings to attend. Since it was New Year's Day, there would be the traditional reception at the White House. And then there was the document that he had promised to sign. It was the Emancipation Proclamation, the legal order that would emancipate, or free, the slaves.

Attending social engagements and issuing important proclamations would have to wait. First, Lincoln had to deal with the business of war. For more than a year and a half, the two sections of the country had been waging a bloody war against each other. The Southern Confederates, or rebels, were fighting so that they might have their own country. Union, or federal, troops from the North were fight-

In the fall of 1862, the federal forces under General Burnside were headed toward Richmond, Virginia, to capture the Confederate capital and end the war. On the way, Burnside planned to attack the Confederates at Fredericksburg, a small town on the southwest bank of the Rappahannock River. While Burnside delayed his attack, Confederate troops dug trenches and made their battle plan. Although outnumbered by 40,000 troops, the Confederates won the battle. The Union lost about 12,500 men, while the Confederates lost about 4,000.

ing to keep the South part of the United States. As commander in chief of the United States, Lincoln was in charge of managing the Northern armies.

Early on this day, General Ambrose E. Burnside, commander of the Army of the Potomac, stood before Lincoln. Burnside had recently lost a battle at Fredericksburg, Virginia. Worse than that, he believed he had lost the confidence of his soldiers. Because it is so important that military leaders have the support of their troops, Burnside asked to be relieved of his command. Lincoln carefully listened to the general, then refused his request. The president had no one to replace Burnside.

At 11 o'clock in the morning, the New Year's Day reception began at the White House. Diplomats and cabinet members, in their horse-drawn carriages, arrived first. Following them came officers of the army and the navy. At noon the general public was admitted.

During the reception President Lincoln greeted hundreds of guests. He made conversation, joked, and shook hands for three hours. After the guests left, Lincoln climbed the stairs to his study. He pulled off his white gloves and rubbed his right hand, which had become swollen from handshaking. It was finally time to put his signature on what would become one of the most important documents in the nation's history.

The Emancipation Proclamation had been on Lincoln's mind for a long time. Several months earlier, in the spring of 1862, he had decided that he would use his special wartime authority to free the slaves. Lincoln wrote the first draft of the Proclamation during his frequent visits to the telegraph room at the War Department, where he spent many hours waiting for the latest news about the war.

When Lincoln spoke with friends and advisers about his plan to free the slaves, he received their support. On July 22 he met with the members of his cabinet and told them about the Proclamation. After Lincoln read it out loud, the cabinet members discussed it and gave their opinions. Edward Bates, the attorney general, liked the Proclamation the way it was. Salmon P. Chase, the secretary of the treasury, thought the army should free the slaves as the Union forces took over areas of the South. Edwin M. Stanton, the secretary of war, supported the Proclamation and thought it should be issued at once. The postmaster general, Montgomery Blair, believed issuing the Proclamation before the fall elections was a political mistake that would cost the president support for the war. Secretary of State William H. Seward favored the idea of the Emancipation Proclamation but suggested the president wait until after a significant Northern victory to announce it. Otherwise, Seward argued, the public might view it as a last, desperate attempt to win the war by starting a slave rebellion.

Lincoln decided to wait for a military success, but a victory did not come soon. First the Union lost at the Second Battle of Bull Run (August 1862). Then word came that Confederate General Robert E. Lee had invaded Maryland and was moving north. The Union needed a victory now more than ever.

As General George McClellan, then commander of the Army of the Potomac, followed the Confederates into Maryland, a Union corporal found three cigars wrapped in paper. On the paper was written Lee's orders to his army. Now McClellan knew where Lee was and what he was planning to do. He knew that Lee had divided his army and was vulnerable to attack.

On September 15 McClellan caught up with Lee at Antietam Creek, near the town of Sharpsburg, Maryland. But instead of attacking with his 95,000 federal troops, McClellan spent two days planning and preparing. This gave Lee time to get help for his army of only 18,000 men.

Finally, McClellan attacked, but by then Lee's troops had more than doubled in number. The battle at Antietam lasted only a day, but it was the bloodiest day of the war. More than 20,000 men were killed or wounded. Although the casualties were nearly the same for both sides, McClellan's army

Lincoln and his cabinet discuss the Emancipation Proclamation. From the left: Secretary of War Edwin M. Stanton, Secretary of the Treasury Salmon P. Chase, President Abraham Lincoln, Secretary of the Navy Gideon Welles, Secretary of State William H. Seward (front), Secretary of the Interior Caleb B. Smith, Postmaster General Montgomery Blair, and Attorney General Edward Bates.

was much larger and could afford more losses. In the end, Antietam was considered a victory for the Union.

Lincoln was unhappy that McClellan had not

The Battle of Antietam, a costly victory for the North, finally gave Lincoln the military success he needed to issue the Preliminary Emancipation Proclamation.

★ ★ ★ ★ ★ ★ ★ ★ ★ ★ ★ ★ ★ ★ ★

Soldiers weren't the only ones whose lives were in danger during battles of the Civil War. Clara Barton, who would later become the founder of the American Red Cross, served as a nurse for sick and wounded soldiers. At Antietam, a bullet ripped through Barton's sleeve, and although she was unhurt, it hit the man she was nursing.

General George McClellan

moved faster and won more decisively, but the Union had the victory Lincoln needed to make his Proclamation public. On September 22, 1862, President Lincoln issued what was known as the Preliminary Emancipation Proclamation, which stated that the Confederates had until January 1, 1863, to make peace. If they did not make peace by then, their slaves would be set free.

Word of the Proclamation spread quickly. Workers at the Government Printing Office made thousands of copies of the preliminary document. They distributed them to government agencies, foreign countries, the press, and the army. Newspapers throughout the North and the South printed the text of the Preliminary Emancipation Proclamation for the public to read.

As the January 1 deadline approached, many people wondered about Lincoln. It was clear he wanted to win the war quickly, but did the president really want to free the slaves? Would he actually sign the Emancipation Proclamation?

Lincoln seemed determined to keep his promise. Nothing short of a Confederate surrender would change the president's mind. And so, on the afternoon of January 1, 1863, Lincoln stood in his study. On the desk before him lay the Emancipation Proclamation, ready for his signature. When Lincoln picked up a pen to sign the document, his

Newspaper editorials varied in their response to the Preliminary Emancipation Proclamation. They ranged from the *New York Times*, which wrote that the Proclamation was the most "important and far-reaching document ever issued since the foundation of this Government," to the *Richmond (Virginia) Enquirer*, which declared the Proclamation to be the "last extremity of wickedness which it was left for our enemy to adopt."

hand and arm began to shake so violently he could not write. He wondered if he might be having second thoughts, but then remembered the hours of handshaking from which he had just come.

Satisfied with the logical explanation for his trembling hand, Lincoln dipped his pen in ink, then paused to say, "I never, in my life, felt more certain that I was doing right than I do in signing this paper." And then, instead of signing *A. Lincoln,* as he usually did, he wrote out his full name: *Abraham Lincoln.* Knowing how important the Proclamation was, Lincoln commented: "If my name ever goes into history, it will be for this act."

In Northern cities thousands of people—both black and white—sang songs, marched in parades, and listened to speeches. In Boston the mayor ordered a 100-gun salute to be fired in honor of the Proclamation. In Hanover, New Hampshire, students at Dartmouth rang the college bell for three hours.

Blacks throughout the South were jubilant. While many had to wait until federal forces won control of their area to gain their freedom, those in Union-held areas could celebrate freely. And they did. At Camp Saxton, South Carolina, the Proclamation was observed by prayer, speeches, and songs. Members of a black volunteer regiment were honored—a fitting tribute to those who were willing to risk their lives in the name of freedom.

The Emancipation Proclamation. Was it really about freedom? Was it issued because of the belief that all people, regardless of their color, are created equal? Or was it signed for a more practical reason, as yet another maneuver on the part of the president to end the Civil War? This book will look at both sides of the question. It will encourage you to decide for yourself about one of the most important documents in the history of the United States.

TWO

Unfair and Unjust

Many people believe the Emancipation Proclamation was issued because slavery was immoral. To better understand this viewpoint, we should examine how slavery developed in the United States.

Slavery did not begin when the first settlers from England arrived in North America in the late 1500s. These colonists, like many of the explorers before them, were looking for gold and other treasures. Instead, all they found was land. But that discovery turned out to be an advantage, because the settlers needed farmland to grow food. It wasn't long before the colonists realized how rich the land was, providing them an opportunity to make their fortunes raising crops, especially tobacco.

The English government, eager to expand its borders, encouraged Britons to move to its Virginia colony. Despite the fact that the area was already occupied by a variety of Native American peoples, England gave colonists the legal right to the land in exchange for the promise that they would settle and farm it. But developing the land was not easy. Landowners needed many laborers to clear and work it.

At first the solution was to send more workers from England. Criminals were released from jails and shipped to the colonies to work. Poor people who owed money were sent to the colonies to pay off their debts. Sometimes people would exchange the cost of the trip to the colonies for their labor. The amount of time individuals worked ranged from four to fourteen years or more, depending on the circumstances. When the length of work was agreed to, a contract was drawn up and then carefully torn in half. The worker took one half; the person for whom he or she was working took the other half. After working the agreed amount of time, the laborer was given the other half of the contract and was free to leave. Because torn, or indented, paper was used, these workers were known as indentured servants.

During the colonial period more than half the people who came to North America from Europe were indentured servants. But even though they arrived in large numbers, still more workers were needed. The colonists tried using Native Americans but were unsuccessful. Native peoples resisted being captured and fought fiercely to remain free. Those who were captured often could escape, because they were familiar with the land and because they had family and friends nearby to help them.

The colonists found the solution to their labor shortage in Africa. It was a common practice there, as in other parts of the world, for warring tribes to take prisoners during battles. These prisoners were used in several different ways. They might be held as hostages to prevent further attacks, or be exchanged for prisoners taken by the enemy. Sometimes prisoners would be used as servants.

European traders saw an opportunity to make money by supplying the labor needed in the colonies. They decided to trade goods to the Africans for prisoners, whom they would then take to the colonies to trade or sell. In a short time African prisoners would become the major source of slave labor in America. There were several reasons for this. Arabs and Europeans had already set up a system for trading African slaves. Also, unlike Native Americans, African slaves were far from home and friends, making escape difficult.

In 1619 Dutch traders brought the first African prisoners to the Virginia Colony and exchanged them for goods. In the beginning, the Africans were

The year 1619 did not mark the first time Africans were forced from their villages and sold. Two hundred years earlier, Portuguese sailors had begun a slave trade when they took Africans to Lisbon, the capital of Portugal. As exploration continued into the Americas, so did the slave trade. By 1619, more than 1 million Africans had been taken to South America as well as the islands of the Caribbean.

An eighteenth-century artist's picture of the slave trade. Europeans traded manufactured goods to Africans in exchange for slaves.

treated as indentured servants and then set free. But it wasn't long before that practice began to change. Laws were passed that protected only the rights of white indentured servants. In some colonies Africans were required to remain servants their entire lives, and even their children had to serve for life. Gradually, African servants became known as slaves.

Slavery became an established practice because it helped certain groups of people become wealthy. Landowners in the colonies depended on slaves to make their farms productive and profitable. European traders saw the opportunity to make money by buying and selling slaves. Shippers could also get rich by transporting African prisoners.

As the demand for slaves rose throughout the colonies, the methods of obtaining them became increasingly brutal. Traders attacked West African villages using guns—weapons the Africans had never seen and could not defend themselves against. Sometimes Africans were given weapons and promised they could remain free as long as they captured other Africans.

For Africans, being captured was the beginning of a nightmare. They were shackled and forced to walk to trading centers that had been constructed along the coast. The journey was difficult and long, sometimes as far as 1,000 miles. Prisoners who tried to escape were whipped or killed. If they survived long enough to make it to the trading centers—and as many as two of five did not—the Africans were put into cages, sold, branded with red-hot irons, then loaded on to waiting ships.

Each ship carried hundreds of prisoners for the voyage to the Americas, which took about a month. The prisoners were jammed onto narrow shelves below the deck, then chained to a railing so they could not move. The area was dark and so crowded that the prisoners often had difficulty breathing. In good weather the crew of the ship took a few prisoners up on deck for fresh air and exercise. Each day they were given water and a handful of either beans or rice mixed with yams to eat. It is not surprising that many of the Africans became seriously ill, and it was not unusual for 10 to 40 percent to die on the journey.

When the ships reached the colonies, the prisoners were unloaded and sold at auctions to farmers or plantation owners. Buyers inspected the Africans as though they were livestock, carefully noting height and weight and even looking into their mouths to check their teeth.

Once sold, the Africans lived their lives at the mercy of their masters. While the conditions of slaves varied, most lived in small, dirt-floor shacks

Booker T. Washington, who became a famous educator and black leader, was born a slave. Like many slave children, Washington began his life of hard work before he was ten years old. His days were spent doing yard work, carrying water to slaves working in the fields, and hauling heavy bags of corn to be ground at the mill. Washington was ordered to follow his master's daughter to school and carry her books. At dinnertime he spent hours fanning flies away from the table as his master's family ate.

and worked from dawn to dusk in the fields. They were not paid for their labor, and they were not permitted to learn to read or write. Anyone who resisted or tried to run away was beaten or sold.

Because of the brutal treatment of slaves, it is not surprising that many people were opposed to slavery. How could it be right to buy and sell human beings? Was it fair to treat people like possessions?

The strongest opposition to slavery came from the slaves themselves. But being at the mercy of others, they were in no position to help themselves. The slaves were in a strange land far from home, were often unable to communicate with one another, and did not have access to weapons. They would need help from the European settlers to become free.

Fortunately, there were colonists who opposed slavery, too. In 1688 Quakers in Pennsylvania protested the use of slaves in their colony. Slavery, they argued, was not consistent with their religious beliefs. In Massachusetts, in 1701, Samuel Sewall, a judge, wrote a pamphlet, entitled *The Selling of Joseph*, which argued against slavery. Sewall was one of the first colonists to publish his antislavery views.

Opposition to slavery grew during the 1700s. When Great Britain began imposing heavy taxes on the colonies in the 1760s, the European settlers

Massachusetts Judge Samuel Sewall, an early opponent of slavery

carefully considered their rights and freedoms. Their thinking led some to consider the rights and freedoms of slaves as well, lending support to the antislavery movement. Benjamin Franklin wrote pamphlets against slavery and helped start the first antislavery society in the colonies. Several free blacks, such as church founder Richard Allen, scientist and mathematician Benjamin Bannecker, and social reformer Prince Hall, wrote and spoke out against slavery.

As time passed, many colonists were ready to break away from Great Britain. For some, declaring their independence seemed the most appropriate time to free slaves as well. Others saw the wrongs of slavery. In an early draft of the Declaration of Independence, Thomas Jefferson criticized the king

Richard Allen, one of the nation's first black activists

of England for participating in the slave trade. He wrote that the king had "waged cruel war against human nature itself, violating its most sacred rights of life & liberty in the persons of a distant people who never offended him, captivating & carrying them into slavery in another hemisphere or to incur miserable death in their transportation thither."

During the Revolutionary War, slaves were enlisted on both sides. After the colonists defeated the British, in 1781, it was time to form a new government. Representatives from each state met to create a constitution, which would provide a foundation for the new country. The delegates discussed a variety of issues, including slavery, and many of the representatives wanted to outlaw it. However, there were powerful and influential men who wanted to keep slavery. In the end, the delegates felt it was more important to form a nation than to argue about slavery.

As the eighteenth century came to a close, many Americans believed that slavery was beginning to die out. The North had little need for slaves, and the fight for independence had created a mood of freedom in many of the newly formed states. During the period between 1781 and 1804, slavery was abolished in New England and in the Middle Atlantic states, and it was banned in the Northwest Territory.

In the Southern states, slaves worked the fields

of cotton, rice, and tobacco, but the sales of these crops often did not cover the costs of buying and taking care of slaves. Cotton was an especially difficult crop to raise because it took a worker a whole day to separate the fiber from the sticky seeds of only one pound of cotton.

It seemed as though slavery's days were numbered. And then, in 1793, along came an invention that changed everything. Teacher and amateur inventor Eli Whitney was visiting in Georgia when he built a simple device that separated the cotton fiber from the seeds. Called the cotton gin (*gin* is short for *engine*), this machine was able to separate up to 1,000 pounds of cotton a day. The cotton gin, along with the development of textile factories in the North, created a huge demand for cotton. Cotton soon became the most important crop in the South, and many workers were needed to pick it.

Despite the growing demand for slaves in cotton-producing states, Congress, in 1808, made it

The cotton gin greatly increased cotton production in the South. In 1790 Southern states were producing 1,000 tons of cotton a year. By 1860 production had increased by a thousand times to 1 million tons per year. During the same period, the slave population grew from 500,000 to 4 million.

Interest in ending slavery was not confined to people in the Northern states. In the early 1800s, there were 143 emancipation societies in the United States; 103 of these societies were located in Southern states.

illegal to import slaves into the United States. This law was the result of a worldwide reform movement in which many nations worked to end slavery.

The 1800s was a time of tremendous growth in the United States. The country added vast expanses of land, pushing its borders all the way west to the Pacific. The population also grew, rising from 8 million in 1800 to 31 million in 1860.

As the United States gained territory, new states were formed and admitted to the Union. To limit the influence of the South and to help prevent the spread of slavery, Congress passed the Missouri Compromise in 1820. This set of laws admitted Missouri as a slave state and Maine as a free state, and then divided western lands into free and slave territories.

In the 1850s people opposed to slavery formed a new political party, the Republicans. The goals of the Republicans were to prevent slavery from spreading and to keep the United States from splitting apart. One man who joined the Republican party soon after it was formed was Abraham Lincoln.

An Illinois lawyer and member of Congress, Lincoln strongly opposed slavery. He believed that blacks were entitled to all the rights set forth in the Declaration of Independence, including the right to life, liberty, and the pursuit of happiness. Slavery,

NEGROES
FOR SALE.

I will sell by Public Auction, on Tuesday of next Court, being the 29th of November, *Eight Valuable Family Servants*, consisting of one Negro Man, a first-rate field hand, one No. 1 Boy, 17 years o' age, a trusty house servant, one excellent Cook, one House-Maid, and one Seamstress. The balance are under 12 years of age. They are sold for no fault, but in consequence of my going to reside North. Also a quantity of Household and Kitchen Furniture, Stable Lot, &c. Terms accommodating, and made known on day of sale.

Jacob August.
P. J. TURNBULL, *Auctioneer.*
Warrenton, October 28, 1859.

Printed at the *News* office, Warrenton, North Carolina.

Posters like this one were not unusual in the days of slavery.

he said, was a "monstrous injustice." For some historians, this was reason enough for Lincoln, when he became president, to have freed the slaves.

THREE

Widespread Prejudice

But was moral indignation the true reason why the slaves were freed? Did people, even President Lincoln himself, really feel that the immorality of slavery was enough reason for it to be abolished?

And why, if slavery was such an evil practice, was it allowed to exist for more than two hundred years? Some historians say that slavery continued for so long because it was an accepted practice and because most people were not disturbed enough to protest it.

In the 1600s and early 1700s, economic interests and prejudice—a belief that blacks were inferior to whites—allowed slavery to take root in the colonies, in both North and South. Prejudice also served as the basis for restricting the rights of blacks who were not slaves. In many states, free blacks could not vote. They could not hold office or serve in the military except as laborers. They could not even

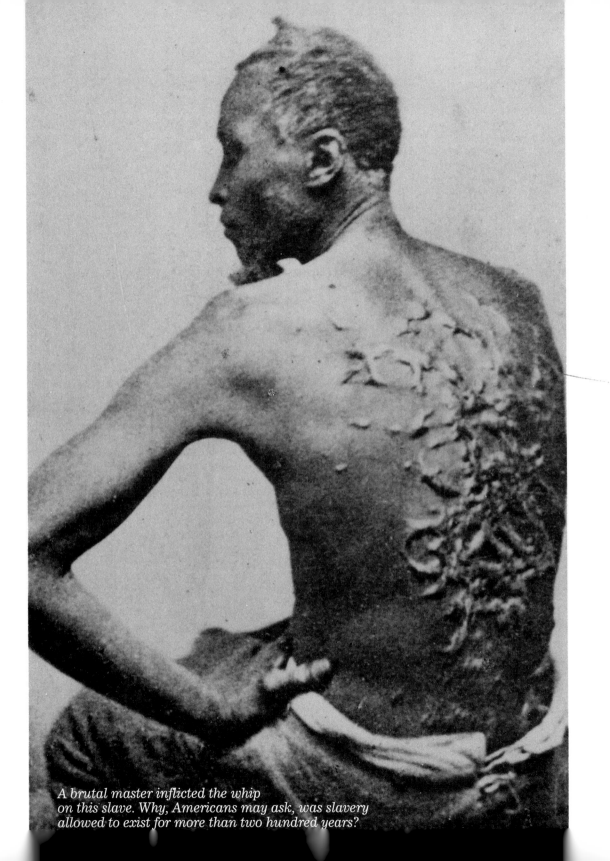

A brutal master inflicted the whip on this slave. Why, Americans may ask, was slavery allowed to exist for more than two hundred years?

enter the state of Indiana. In the South, free blacks had to carry special papers issued by the courts. Those caught without their papers were jailed, forced to work, or sold.

Slavery was such an accepted part of life that even people who spoke out against it were involved with slaves. Benjamin Franklin, who founded the first antislavery society, owned several slaves during his lifetime and printed advertisements for slave auctions in his newspaper. George Washington not only considered slavery an evil in itself but also believed that it was bad for the country. Yet he owned more than three hundred slaves. James Madison and James Monroe, too, were both slaveholders and critics of slavery.

And consider Thomas Jefferson, who declared, "All men are created equal." His early drafts of the Declaration of Independence included strong criticisms of slavery, but he consented to strike out those parts so that the document would receive Southern support. And while Jefferson worked hard to limit and even put an end to slavery, he was the owner of more than five hundred slaves.

When Northern states began to abolish slavery around the beginning of the nineteenth century, they were not especially concerned with morality. Instead, their action was more a reflection of their economic needs. Unlike the South, the North had a

Prejudice against blacks can even be seen in the efforts to free them. Colonization was a popular plan among those opposed to slavery. In this plan, blacks—free as well as slave—would be sent out of the country to start their own colony. Thomas Jefferson proposed a colonization plan as early as 1776. The American Colonization Society was formed, and Virginians James Madison and James Monroe served as two of its presidents. During its first twenty years, the society sent four thousand blacks to a settlement on the west coast of Africa that became the nation of Liberia in 1824.

temperate climate and rocky terrain. It was more suited to factories than farms, and factory owners had not much need for slaves. They preferred to hire immigrants, whom they could pay low wages— and fire when they weren't needed.

The South, with its warm climate and rich soil, was much more suitable for agriculture. Its crops— cotton, sugar, and tobacco—relied heavily on slave labor. To many Southerners, slavery may have been an evil, but it was a necessary evil.

Conflict resulted from the differences between the industrial North and the agricultural South. In the early 1800s, Southern farmers shipped their cotton to English factories, where it was made into clothing. Then the clothing was sent back to the United States to be sold. When Congress charged tariffs, or fees, on the clothing coming into the United States, the English produced less clothing and bought less cotton. The decrease in demand helped lower the price of cotton for Northern factory owners, who became more successful. Cotton growers complained about the tariffs but could not reduce them, because the North had the larger population and therefore more votes in Congress.

As the North continued to grow and industrialize, Southerners became concerned. They worried about the power of the North and believed that Southern interests were not being met. Some feared the North would pass laws that would change their way of life, including the ownership of slaves. But even when the importation of slaves was made

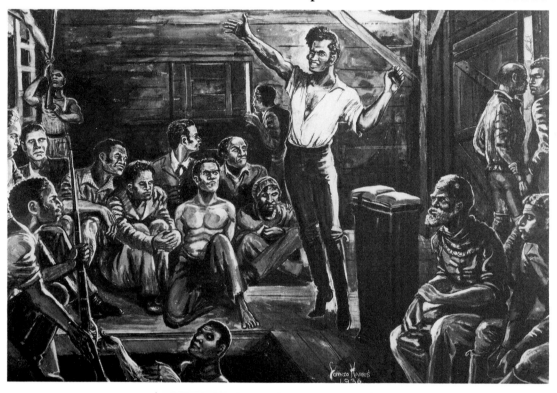

Nearly one hundred years after Nat Turner's rebellion, an artist drew a fiery scene of the rebel urging his fellow slaves to revolt.

★
★
★
★
★
★
★
★
★
★
★
★
★

Southerners were concerned about more than slavery being outlawed. Many feared that the slaves would revolt. In 1829, David Walker, a free black clothing dealer in Boston, published *An Appeal to the Colored Citizens of the World.* In this pamphlet, Walker urged slaves to use violence against their masters. "Kill," he said, "or be killed."

Nat Turner was a slave who wanted to liberate his people. In the summer of 1831, Turner led seventy slaves in a revolt against a Virginia community. The slaves killed about fifty-five whites before they were captured and executed. Turner's rebellion left Southerners terrified of a slave uprising and caused an outbreak of violence against blacks. More than two hundred slaves were killed to set an example for other blacks.

illegal in 1808, the practice continued, and more than ten thousand Africans were brought into the United States illegally each year.

Generally, most people in the North did not care one way or the other about slavery. There were some who opposed it in a mild way; they criticized the practice and did not want it to spread to new states entering the Union. A few other people were outraged by the evils of slavery. They wanted to end the practice immediately, and they became known as abolitionists.

One of the most famous abolitionists was William Lloyd Garrison. Garrison believed slavery was evil, that slave owners were sinners, and that the practice of slavery had to be stopped at once. In 1831 Garrison founded *The Liberator*, an abolitionist newspaper. In the first edition of *The Liberator*, Garrison made his intentions about slavery clear. He wrote: "On this subject, I do not wish to think or speak, or write with moderation. Tell a man whose house is on fire to give a moderate alarm. . . . I am in earnest. I will not equivocate. I will not excuse. I

The Liberator's *first masthead, published in April 1831*

will not retreat a single inch. AND I WILL BE HEARD."

The public did not support the abolitionists' strong views. In the South, many post offices refused to deliver abolitionist newspapers. The state of Georgia offered a $5,000 reward to anyone who would bring Garrison to trial.

Opposition was not limited to the South. In 1853, when Garrison arranged to have an English abolitionist speak in Boston, a mob of at least five thousand tried to tar and feather Garrison. He escaped unharmed, but abolitionists in other areas were not so fortunate. Antiabolitionist riots were held in most large Northern cities. Abolitionists were beaten, and some were even killed during these protests.

Children whose parents were abolitionists participated in the antislavery movement. They read antislavery books and magazines, learned songs, attended lectures with their parents, and joined

Abolitionists taught their children that slavery was wrong. At right are two pages from The Anti-Slavery Alphabet, *a children's book published in 1847.*

A is an Abolitionist—
A man who wants to free
The wretched slave—and give to all
An equal liberty.

B is a Brother with a skin
Of somewhat darker hue,
But in our Heavenly Father's sight,
He is as dear as you.

5

C is the Cotton-field, to which
This injured brother's driven,
When, as the white man's *slave*, he toils
From early morn till even.

D is the Driver, cold and stern,
Who follows, whip in hand,
To punish those who dare to rest,
Or disobey command.

★ ★ ★ ★ ★ ★ ★ ★ ★ ★ ★ ★ ★ ★ ★

Harriet Tubman

The Underground Railroad was a network of people who helped slaves escape to freedom in the North. The most famous "conductor" of the Underground Railroad was Harriet Tubman, a woman who had once been a slave. Tubman made nineteen trips into the South to help slaves escape. The trips were dangerous, and she had to use every bit of bravery and cunning to keep from getting caught. Once she disguised herself as a man and drove a wagon of slaves hidden under a load of manure. The slaves breathed through straws that stuck out of the manure.

Another former slave, Frederick Douglass, also fought hard to end slavery. Born in 1817, Douglass escaped to the North with his wife in 1838. Three years later he was asked to talk about his experiences as a slave. He spoke so intelligently that some people found it hard to believe that he had ever been a slave. To answer their doubts, he wrote a book about his life.

After living in England for a few years to protect himself from his former owner, Douglass moved to Rochester, New York, in 1847. There he started a newspaper called the *North Star*. The paper was named after the North Star, in the Little Dipper, which runaway slaves followed as they made their way north. In his newspaper, Douglass called for equal rights for blacks as well as for Native Americans and women.

Frederick Douglass

junior antislavery societies. Some children assisted their families in helping slaves run away on the Underground Railroad.

Despite the great efforts by abolitionists, there was little public support for ending slavery. In the North, only one of every twenty people was part of the abolitionist movement. Prejudice against blacks was widespread. The general feeling among most Northerners was that slavery did not affect them and they did not need to be concerned about it.

In the South there was great resistance to ending slavery. For plantation owners, the slaves represented an enormous investment: $2 billion worth of property. These Southerners were not about to forfeit willingly what they considered to be rightfully theirs. Two-thirds of the whites in the South did not own slaves, and freed slaves meant increased job competition for many of them. For all Southerners, if slavery were abolished, their traditional way of life would change forever.

Given the attitude among most Americans in the mid-1800s, we should not be surprised at the laws that were passed and the court decisions that were handed down then. In 1850 the Fugitive Slave Act made it a federal crime to help or hide a runaway slave. Under the Kansas-Nebraska Act of 1854, slavery could expand into western states, because residents of new territories would be allowed to decide for themselves whether or not to permit slavery. In 1857 the U.S. Supreme Court ruled against Dred Scott, a slave who had sued for his freedom after his master took him into a free territory. The decision also ruled that the Missouri Compromise

$100 REWARD

Ran away from the subscriber, living near the Anacostia Bridge, on or about the 17th November, negro girl ELIZA. She calls herself Eliza Coursy. She is of the ordinary size, from 18 to 20 years old, of a chestnut or copper color. Eliza has some scars about her face, has been hired in Washington, and has acquaintances in Georgetown.

I will give fifty dollars if taken in the District or Maryland, and one hundred dollars if taken in any free State ; but in either case she must be secured in jail so that I get her again.

JOHN. P. WARING.

Nov. 28, 1857.

H. Polkinhorn's Steam Job Printing Office, D street, bet. 6th & 7th sts., Washington, D. C.

★ ★ ★ ★

When Congress passed the Fugitive Slave Act to help Southern slaveholders, it put the United States government in the business of catching runaway slaves. The government paid federal agents and private citizens to hunt down escaped slaves. But some "slave hunters" did not limit themselves to catching runaways. They kidnapped free blacks and claimed rewards for them, too.

In this advertisement, a slave owner offers a reward for a young runaway. Under the Fugitive Slave Act of 1850, it was a federal crime to help an escaped slave.

was unconstitutional and that blacks, both free and slave, were not citizens and did not have the right to sue in court.

Slavery was becoming the focal point of the conflict, which was based on economics and political power, between North and South. After proslavery and antislavery settlers in the Kansas Territory fought and killed each other during 1855 and 1856, Senator Charles Sumner of Massachusetts delivered a two-day speech against the slavery movement in Kansas. He sharply criticized other senators who supported slavery.

Two days later, as Sumner sat writing letters at his desk in the Senate chamber, he was attacked by Preston Brooks, a member of Congress from South Carolina and a relative of one of the men Sumner had criticized. Brooks beat Sumner over and over with his gold-headed cane until the Massachusetts senator was bleeding and seriously injured. Three years went by before Sumner recovered enough from his injuries to return to the Senate. Brooks, who became a hero in the South, was fined only $300 for the attack.

Not even Abraham Lincoln, who publicly opposed slavery, can be seen as fully committed to change. Lincoln, who in 1857 was practicing law, spoke out against slavery. Nevertheless, he supported the idea of sending blacks out of the country to start a colony of their own. In court cases he defended the owners of fugitive slaves and backed Southerners' rights to their "property."

For Lincoln, maintaining the unity of the nation appears to have been the most important goal. His primary concern, it seems, was that the growing split between the North and the South be healed. As early as June 1858, during his speech to accept the Republican nomination to run for the Senate, he said that the arguments about slavery "will not cease until a crisis shall have been reached and passed. A house divided against itself cannot stand. I believe this government cannot endure permanently half slave and half free. I do not expect the Union to be dissolved—I do not expect the house to fall—but I do expect it will cease to be divided. It will become all one thing, or all the other."

FOUR

A Moderate Approach

Abraham Lincoln was not an abolitionist. Although he was opposed to slavery, he believed that putting an immediate end to slavery would cause many serious problems. He also believed that the president's power to end slavery was restricted by the Constitution. Lincoln was one of many moderates who wanted to limit slavery and who felt that slavery would die out on its own. His moderate views enabled him to make compromises and wait.

Lincoln was a practical politician. He knew that in order to make changes in society, he would have to get elected and that getting elected required voter support. Lincoln knew that his best chance of appealing to the voters was to hold moderate rather than extreme public views. Extreme views and actions, according to moderates like Lincoln, often worked to delay progress and change.

John Brown's raid on the arsenal at Harpers Ferry ended in disaster when slaves in the surrounding area failed to support the rebels.

★ ★ ★ ★ ★ ★ ★ ★ ★ ★ ★ ★ ★ ★

One extremist was John Brown. A Connecticut-born abolitionist, Brown had been opposed to slavery since he was a youth. He based his views on his strong religious beliefs. He became nationally known during the conflict over slavery in Kansas when he was found responsible for killing five proslavery settlers. He later moved east and developed a plan to end slavery by leading a slave rebellion.

Brown's plan was for him and his followers to capture weapons at the federal arsenal at Harpers Ferry, Virginia. He would give the weapons to slaves, who, he believed, would join his uprising. His army of slaves would then march through the South, freeing slaves wherever they went.

On the night of October 16, 1859, Brown and twenty-one followers, including three of his sons, took over the arsenal at Harpers Ferry. They took hostages and then waited for the word of their raid to spread to slaves living in the area.

Word of John Brown's raid spread quickly throughout the countryside, but it did not have the effect Brown had hoped. Slaves, concerned for the safety of themselves and their families, failed to rally to his side. Instead, townspeople and marines surrounded the arsenal and overpowered the raiders, taking Brown and four followers as prisoners. All the others were dead or had escaped. After a hasty trial, the raiders who had been captured were sentenced to be executed. On December 2, 1859, John Brown and his four followers were hanged.

John Brown

The subject of slavery was on the minds of millions of voters during the presidential election of 1860. The Republicans, who had campaigned strongly against slavery in 1856 and lost the election by more than a two-to-one margin, changed their public views on slavery. This time they were more moderate in their opposition. The party leaders rejected a prominent politician, Senator William Seward of New York, who claimed there could be no compromising when it came to ending slavery. Instead, the Republicans selected as their candidate a man who better represented their moderate viewpoint: Abraham Lincoln.

Although his views about slavery were moderate, not everyone thought so. Abolitionists saw him as weak and unwilling to take a strong stand. To Southerners, his views were dangerous and radical. Immediately after Lincoln was elected, and more than two months before he was to take office, South Carolina seceded from the United States. Six Southern states followed, basing their decision on the election of a president "whose opinions and purposes are hostile to slavery."

Representatives of the Southern states met at Montgomery, Alabama, during the first week of February 1861. They created a constitution and a new nation: the Confederate States of America. The representatives selected Jefferson Davis, from

Jefferson Davis, president of the Confederacy

Mississippi, as their president and Alexander H. Stevens, of Georgia, as their vice president.

Lincoln hoped for a compromise that would bring the Confederate states back into the Union. He appealed to them in his inauguration speech on March 4. He also warned them of his plan to live up to his oath as president to "preserve, protect, and defend" the United States. Indeed, he was determined to preserve the Union at all costs.

Within a month of Lincoln's inauguration, a crisis developed in South Carolina. Fort Sumter, which lay in Charleston harbor, was controlled by federal soldiers. Since the people of South Carolina believed they were no longer in the United States,

The war that took place within the United States from 1861 to 1865 is known by more than thirty different names. Official U.S. records call it the War of the Rebellion. People in the North and South have referred to it by a variety of titles, depending on their viewpoint. The conflict has been called the Civil War, the War for the Preservation of the Union, the Brothers' War, Mr. Lincoln's War, the War Between the States, the War Against Northern Aggression, the War for States' Rights, the War for Constitutional Liberty, and the War for Southern Independence.

Not only did the name of the war vary—many of the battles were known by different names as well.

their governor demanded that the U.S. Army surrender the fort. When the fort's commander, Major Robert Anderson, refused, the Confederates opened fire. The shots became the official beginning of the armed conflict between the states.

When Lincoln learned that Union forces had surrendered Fort Sumter to the Confederates, he was not overly concerned. The North, he believed, would stop the rebellion quickly. After all, the Union had twenty-three states with 22 million people on its side. Although three more states had joined the Confederacy, the South had only eleven states and 9 million people, 4 million of whom were slaves. The North had many factories to produce weapons and ammunition, railroads to transport troops, and a strong navy to blockade Southern ports. The advantages for the South were its strong will to fight for its independence and its talented military leaders.

On April 15, Lincoln issued a request for 75,000 volunteers, who would each serve ninety days. That would be enough time to crush the South, Lincoln thought. In the spring and into the summer of 1861, commanders from both the North and the South organized and trained their armies. It wasn't until the morning of July 21 that the armies met for a major battle. The setting was a small, muddy stream called Bull Run, on the outskirts of Manassas,

Virginia. The result was a disorganized and bloody battle (called Bull Run by the North and Manassas by the South) in which chaos and then panic developed among Union soldiers, causing them to drop their weapons and run. Instead of easily defeating the outnumbered rebels, the Northern troops were routed.

While the South celebrated its victory, the North began to look at the war in realistic terms. The conflict was not going to be as short and as easy as the Northerners had expected. It would, instead, be long, difficult, and bloody. Lincoln, realizing the challenge before him, called up more troops for longer enlistments, tightened the naval blockade of the South, and ordered his commanders to launch attacks on three areas of the South.

As the war progressed, Lincoln did not change his views about slavery. He still thought it was wrong, but he believed his first obligation was to win the war. Again, a moderate approach seemed the best tactic. Slaveholding states—Delaware, Kentucky, Maryland, and Missouri—formed the border between North and South. These states supported the Northern effort to restore the Union, but they opposed any attempt to free the slaves. Lincoln feared that if he went too fast in working to emancipate the slaves, these border states might join the Confederacy.

Many Northerners expected the Union forces to win the conflict at Bull Run easily. In fact, some people thought the battle would be entertaining. Hundreds of people from Washington, D.C., including members of Congress and their families, traveled the twenty-five miles to Bull Run in carriages, wagons, and buggies and on horseback. They feasted on picnic lunches, drank champagne, and watched the action through opera glasses from hillsides near the battlefield.

So Lincoln devised a voluntary plan to free the slaves, hoping that it would be acceptable to slaveholders. Slaves would be gradually freed over a thirty-year period, and their owners would be paid $500 for each freed slave. This plan would be tested in Delaware, then used in the other border states. Eventually it would go into effect in the South.

Lincoln's Delaware Plan was not even tried because no one in the state legislature would sponsor it. But that did not stop Lincoln. In March 1862 he sent a message to Congress, proposing a similar plan for the border states. When some in Congress complained about the cost of such a program, Lincoln told them that all the slaves in the border states could be bought for the price of fighting the war for eighty-seven days. He assured them that this plan would shorten the war by much more than eighty-seven days.

Lincoln had Republican support for his plan, but he needed the backing of border-state congressmen to get their states to act. He met with members of Congress from the border states on March 10, hoping to convince them of the importance of his plan. But they were not interested in accepting any plan that would eliminate slavery.

Lincoln warned these representatives that the longer the war lasted, the more likely all slavery would be eliminated. He suggested that they take advantage of getting money for their slaves. If they waited too long, Lincoln said, the slaves would be freed and their owners would get nothing. Still, the congressmen would not budge.

Lincoln did the best he could with the support he had. By the summer of 1862, his plan for gradual emancipation had been approved by Congress. He had also signed into law bills that abolished slavery in the District of Columbia, prevented slavery in the territories, and made it illegal for Union officers to return fugitive slaves to the Confederacy. Free blacks were allowed to serve in both the army and the navy, and slaves who volunteered for the armed forces were given their freedom.

Still, many people felt Lincoln was not doing enough for the slaves. These people would not be satisfied unless the slaves were immediately freed. They met with Lincoln, wrote letters, and organized rallies to pressure him to move more quickly. But Lincoln could not be rushed or pressured. He had the entire nation to think about, and he wasn't about to risk the fate of that nation to assist one group of people. So he waited. He waited until the time for emancipation seemed right. He waited until there was a good chance for its success. And then he acted.

FIVE

Desperate for Victory

By the time Lincoln did free the slaves, on January 1, 1863, some people thought he'd taken too long and that he'd issued the Proclamation more to win the war than to end an immoral practice. In his inauguration speech nearly two years earlier, on March 4, 1861, Lincoln could have led the way in opposing slavery. He could have told the nation that this unjust practice would soon be ended for the good of all. Instead, Lincoln tried to soothe the angry feelings of Southerners when he said: "I have no purpose, directly or indirectly, to interfere with the institution of slavery in states where it exists. I believe I have no lawful right to do so, and I have no inclination to do so."

At the same time, Lincoln spoke of his intention to enforce the Fugitive Slave Act, a law which promised slaveholders that the federal government

General Butler

would help capture runaway slaves. He also gave his public support for a bill, passed two days earlier, that made it illegal for Congress to interfere with slavery in the states. If approved by two-thirds of the states, this bill would become an amendment to the Constitution.

Abraham Lincoln was not responsible for the first freeing of slaves during the war. It was an abolitionist, General Benjamin F. Butler, commander of Fortress Monroe, Virginia. In May 1861, when it was illegal for blacks to serve in the Union army, three slaves entered General Butler's camp and asked for protection. The Union general put them to work with the rest of his men.

After Butler accepted the three slaves in his camp, he sent word of his action to Washington, where it was approved by Secretary of War Simon Cameron. Within a few weeks, Congress made the practice official. It passed a law stating that slaves belonging to someone who resisted the laws of the United States could be legally taken from their master. Most Union generals, however, ignored the new law. Lincoln did nothing to enforce it.

A few months later, on August 30, another general tried to take Butler's action a step further. When Major General John C. Frémont took command of the Union forces in Missouri, he declared martial law and issued an emancipation proclama-

General Butler was known as "Beast" Butler to Southerners because of the harsh treatment he used toward them. One of his acts was to have a Confederate hanged for ripping up an American flag. In 1863, when blacks were finally able to serve as soldiers in the Union army, many commanders were reluctant to use them. But not Butler. A strong abolitionist, he felt that black soldiers had more at stake in the war and would fight harder than white soldiers. As a result, he commanded many black troops into battle.

tion. The proclamation granted freedom to all slaves owned by anyone in Missouri who was either fighting or helping people fight against the United States. Lincoln quickly overruled the proclamation.

Abolitionists worked hard during the fall and early winter of 1861 to convince Lincoln to issue a proclamation that would free the slaves. But Lincoln refused. He was afraid to risk losing the support of the slaveholding border states. Still, abolitionists kept pressuring Lincoln and adding practical arguments.

Freeing the slaves, abolitionists argued, would weaken the Confederates' ability to fight. And, after all, wasn't slavery at the heart of the conflict? Slavery was the main reason Southern states had left the Union, it was the cause for the fighting, and it was now serving as the foundation for the Confederacy. It would be ridiculous, they argued, to fight a war without attacking its cause. And what would happen if the war ended before the issue of slavery was resolved? Wouldn't there still be conflict between North and South?

Abolitionists also pointed out the influence an emancipation proclamation would have on foreign countries. Making the elimination of slavery a war objective would make it more difficult for the rebels to get help. Countries like Great Britain, which had ended slavery in the 1830s, would be much less likely to assist the Confederacy if the United States was officially opposed to slavery.

Some of the pressure to free the slaves came from within Lincoln's own administration. Secretary of War Cameron suggested that the president recruit black soldiers to help with the war effort, but Lincoln refused. He did not want any blacks fighting in states that permitted slavery; he could not risk the loss of border-state support.

Lincoln continued to resist abolitionist pressures. He would not free the slaves immediately, but instead proposed the Delaware Plan, which would free slaves over a thirty-year period and compensate slave owners for the loss of their slaves. But what would happen to the freed slaves? Where would they go? What would they do? Lincoln's answer was the same as Thomas Jefferson's: colonize them. Freed slaves and other blacks would be sent to U.S. colonies set up in Central America or Africa. In his annual message to Congress on December 3, 1861, Lincoln asked for funds to carry out his colonization program.

Despite the pressure from abolitionists, all Lincoln offered was another gradual emancipation plan. In the spring of 1862 a colonization program to get blacks out of the country was again closely tied to the plan. To help the colonization efforts, Lincoln and Congress officially recognized the

Abolitionists tried hard to influence the president whenever they had a chance. One day, while Lincoln sat in the Senate gallery, Massachusetts Senator Charles Sumner was giving a speech about Edward Baker, a former Illinois politician and friend of Lincoln's. Baker had recently been killed in battle at Ball's Bluff, a 100-foot bank along the Potomac River in Virginia. In an emotional speech about the loss of Baker, Sumner looked directly at Lincoln and claimed that slavery was the "murderer of our dead senator." A reporter sitting by Lincoln noted that when Lincoln heard these words, he jerked as if he had been stabbed with a knife.

countries of Haiti and Liberia.

While Lincoln continued to move slowly in his efforts to settle the slavery issue, others did not. On May 9, 1862, General David Hunter, who commanded Union forces occupying islands off South Carolina, issued a military order that freed the slaves in South Carolina, Georgia, and Florida. Stating that no military commander had the authority to issue such an order, Lincoln immediately reversed the order. The president, and no one else, would be the one to decide when such an order would be issued. And, according to Lincoln, it would be issued only if it was necessary to save the country.

The war, meanwhile, continued. Early in 1862, Union navy gunboats forced the surrender of Fort Henry in Tennessee. Twelve miles to the east, Union forces under the command of Brigadier General Ulysses S. Grant took control of Fort Donelson.

At Fort Donelson, Grant surrounded the 15,000 Confederates with his 27,000 troops and ordered navy gunboats to fire. The trapped Confederates tried to escape but failed. Finally, Confederate Brigadier General Simon B. Buckner, who had been a friend of Grant's since their days at West Point, asked for surrender terms. He hoped that Grant would allow the Confederates to go home if they promised not to fight again. Grant's response: "No terms except unconditional and immediate surrender can be accepted. I propose to move immediately upon your works." Because of his response, Ulysses S. Grant became known as "Unconditional Surrender" Grant.

General Ulysses S. Grant, seated, with his men

The Union won more victories as the weeks passed. Its forces defended land in the New Mexico Territory against rebel attacks. Grant won a major victory at Shiloh, in Tennessee. General John Pope took Southern strongholds in Missouri. Admiral David Farragut captured New Orleans. The Union navy attacked coastal forts, offshore islands, and stopped the *Virginia*, the South's powerful ironclad ship.

The summer of 1862, however, brought new hope for a Confederate victory. Robert E. Lee, a military adviser to President Jefferson Davis, had been chosen to lead the Confederate Army of Northern

Virginia after Joseph E. Johnston was wounded in battle. It didn't take Lee long to prove himself a brilliant commander.

Badly outnumbered, Lee's forces pushed McClellan's army away from Richmond. While McClellan withdrew his troops to Washington, Lee went on to capture the federal supply base at Manassas Junction, site of the first major battle of the war. Union troops led by General Pope attacked Lee, but they were driven back. Lee was now ready to invade the North.

General Robert E. Lee

Lincoln followed the battles closely, hoping for an end to the bloodshed. But as Confederate victories mounted, Lincoln realized that he would need to do something drastic to help the North win the war. The country was in danger of being divided forever. It was time to save the Union. It was time to free the slaves.

Although his moderate ideas about the slavery issue had not changed, Lincoln had been working on a federal emancipation plan throughout the summer. The plan shouldn't be made public, Lincoln believed, at a time when the North appeared to be close to defeat. He didn't want the public to know that the plan represented a desperate measure.

Horace Greeley, an abolitionist and editor of the *New York Tribune*, wrote a public letter to Lincoln in August 1862. In it Greeley criticized Lincoln's lack of action on the slavery issue. Greeley charged that Lincoln was being influenced too much by politicians from the border states. Then he appealed to Lincoln in practical terms, telling him that the North could use more people—namely, former slaves—to help win the war.

In his reply, Lincoln wrote: "My paramount object in this struggle is to save the Union, and is not either to save or destroy slavery. If I could save the Union without freeing any slave, I would do it; and if I could do it by freeing all the slaves, I would do it;

Journalist Horace Greeley wanted an immediate end to slavery.

and if I could do it by freeing some and leaving others alone, I would also do that. What I do about slavery and the colored race, I do because it helps save this Union; and what I forbear, I forbear because I do not believe it will help save the Union."

That same month, Lincoln invited a group of black leaders to the White House, the first time in history that blacks officially met with the president to talk about a public issue. After discussing the differences between the races, Lincoln proposed that the leaders help recruit volunteers to start colonies of blacks outside the United States. The leaders agreed to help. Other black leaders, hearing of this support for the president's plan, were critical. Some started petitions asking Lincoln to colonize slaveholders instead of blacks.

More pressure came from overseas. The U.S. minister to Vienna, after visiting Paris, London, and Berlin, reported that European countries would soon recognize the Confederate States of America. European support for the Southern cause would prolong the war. The minister reported that recognition could be avoided if the Union soon won a major battle, or if the slaves were freed.

Finally, in September 1862, after the Union victory at Antietam, in Maryland, Lincoln issued the Preliminary Emancipation Proclamation. It is clear, though, that the presidential act did not stem from Lincoln's personal feelings about slavery but rather from his desire to win the war and save the Union. Why else would he have waited so long? Why else would he have delayed until the South appeared to be successful? And, most important, why did he free slaves only in the Southern states? Slaves in areas loyal to the United States were not affected by the Emancipation Proclamation. If Lincoln had truly been concerned about equality, many people believe, he would have freed all the slaves.

SIX

What Do You Think?

The announcement that slaves had been freed did not automatically free them. Most slaveholders ignored the Proclamation, since they believed the president of the United States had no authority over them. Slaves learned about the Proclamation in many different ways. A few read about it in the newspapers. Some overheard white people talking about it. Many found out from Union soldiers who were taking possession of Confederate territory.

Although the Emancipation Proclamation did not free any slaves immediately, it did raise the hopes of blacks throughout both the North and the South. The order also made it possible for blacks to enlist in the Union forces. Although many blacks were already serving in the army and the navy—mainly in noncombat positions—they were to be recognized by the government and given benefits similar to white soldiers'. After the Emancipation Proclamation, they could officially join the fight.

Response to the idea of enlisting black soldiers was mixed in the North. Some, who believed the purpose of the war was to restore the Union, thought that blacks should not be allowed to fight in a war that had little to do with them. Others believed that the war was really about freedom for all people, and they supported the use of black troops.

Southerners were outraged when they heard that the North was going to enlist black soldiers. Not only did the new policy make more troops available to the North; it also meant that every slave was a potential gun-carrying enemy. Confederate President Jefferson Davis, who strongly opposed the use of black soldiers by the North, announced a new prisoner policy: Blacks captured by Confederates would be treated as slaves and either returned to their masters or sold. He suggested that white officers who led black troops be tried as criminals and sentenced to death.

Some Southerners wanted the treatment of captured black soldiers to be more harsh as an example to other blacks. Editorials in Richmond newspapers declared that captured black soldiers should not be taken as prisoners; they should be killed.

By the spring of 1863, it became clear to the

Although blacks were allowed to enlist as soldiers, they were not treated the same as white soldiers. Black soldiers, officially called "colored troops," were restricted to serving in all-black regiments, almost all of which were led by white officers. Black soldiers were given the worst equipment and uniforms, if any at all. They were assigned the lowest types of duties: cleaning latrines, digging earthworks, and serving guard duty. Their pay was half that of white soldiers.

After Northerners became subject to the draft, many men were glad to let blacks take their place in battle. This is an advertisement urging black men to enlist.

leaders in the North that they would need more soldiers to continue the war. In March, Congress passed a law that gave the federal government the power to conscript, or draft, men into the armed forces. Prior to this time only a few states had the draft. The new law helped change the minds of many in the North who were against using black soldiers. Now that they were subject to being called to duty, many were willing to let blacks take their places on the dangerous field of battle.

The first draft took place in July 1863, when President Lincoln called for 300,000 new troops. Men between the ages of 20 and 45 were eligible to be drafted, and they were chosen through a lottery. The names of selected men were printed in newspapers.

The draft did more than raise the number of soldiers for the Union army; it increased tensions among Northerners. Poor people felt it was unfair to them, since a man with money who was drafted could hire a substitute or pay a fee so he wouldn't have to serve. Some whites, angry that the purpose of the war appeared to be to free the slaves, put the blame on blacks. As a result of these tensions, draft riots broke out in Northern cities during the summer of 1863.

In New York City, white rioters set fire to the draft office, attacked the mayor's home, and rampaged the city, burning and looting as they went. Blacks were beaten and lynched. Their homes and property were smashed. Even an orphanage for black children was burned to the ground. By the time federal troops could restore order, more than one hundred people had been killed.

As 1863 came to a close, some people hoped that Lincoln would cancel the Emancipation Procla-

This memorial to the Fifty-fourth Massachusetts Regiment stands in Boston today.

The summer of 1863 was important for the black soldiers in the Union army. Earlier in the year, Massachusetts Governor John A. Andrew had formed the Fifty-fourth Massachusetts Volunteer Infantry Regiment. Andrew appointed Colonel Robert Gould Shaw commander of the regiment and Lieutenant Colonel Edward N. Hallowell as second in command. Both men were white, and both came from well-known abolitionist families.

The Fifty-fourth Massachusetts was the first of many black units to see heavy action during the war. On July 18, 1863, the regiment led the assault on Fort Wagner, a Confederate earthwork that defended the entrance to Charleston harbor in South Carolina. Although the difficult assault was not successful and the infantry regiment lost nearly half its men, including Colonel Shaw, the courage of this unit helped change the minds of many people about black soldiers' ability and willingness to fight. (In 1990, the movie *Glory* was made about the Fifty-fourth Volunteer Infantry Regiment.)

mation. But in his annual message to Congress, Lincoln made it very clear that he would not. "While in my present position," he said, "I shall not attempt to retract or modify the Emancipation Proclamation; nor shall I return to slavery any person who is free by the terms of the Proclamation; or by any acts of Congress."

Many people, including Lincoln himself, doubted whether the Proclamation was legal in freeing slaves forever. Because it was not clear whether the president of the United States had the authority to do this, a constitutional amendment was introduced into the House of Representatives in December 1863. The amendment would prohibit slavery forever in the United States and its territories. After being bitterly debated in the House, the amendment failed to pass by the two-thirds majority it needed. Slavery was still legal in the border states.

Despite Union victories, the war dragged on for more than a year. And then on April 9, 1865, General Robert E. Lee, hopelessly surrounded by Union forces, surrendered to General Ulysses S. Grant. Soon after, other Confederate armies surrendered to the Union. The war was finally over!

People in the North did not celebrate their victory for long. On the evening of April 14, 1865, an actor named John Wilkes Booth slipped into the presidential box and shot Lincoln as he watched a

The costs of the war were tremendous. Billions of dollars were spent by both the North and the South during the four years of conflict. More than 600,000 soldiers lost their lives, but only a third of them had died as a result of enemy weapons. The remaining 400,000 had died of illnesses, including chicken pox, diarrhea, dysentery, malaria, measles, mumps, smallpox, typhoid fever, and yellow fever.

play called *Our American Cousin* at Ford's Theater in Washington. Lincoln died the next day, making him the first American president to be assassinated.

Americans struggled with the loss of their president as well as with the challenging task of rebuilding the nation after four years of death and destruction. For blacks, this period of rebuilding was a time of hope. Slavery became illegal in December 1865 when the Thirteenth Amendment to the Constitution was ratified (accepted by the states). The Fourteenth Amendment, which promised blacks equal rights, was ratified in 1868. And then, two years later, the Fifteenth Amendment, giving black male citizens the right to vote, was ratified.

The fight against slavery was over, but the fight for equality was just beginning. Although slaves had been freed, many whites still believed that black people were inferior. These racist beliefs have been passed down for generations in some communities and families. As a result, blacks have been discriminated against, segregated, intimidated, threatened, and even murdered since the days of the Civil War. Their struggle for equality continues to this day.

The Emancipation Proclamation is one of America's most treasured documents. But why was it issued? What was the real reason slaves were set free?

Those who believe that Lincoln issued the

Proclamation in order to end an evil, unjust practice make several points to support their view:

1. President Lincoln's words show that, personally, he was strongly opposed to slavery.

2. Lincoln signed into law bills that abolished slavery in the District of Columbia, prevented slavery in the territories, and made it illegal to return fugitive slaves to their owners.

3. Lincoln tried hard to convince border-state leaders to support his plan for gradually freeing the slaves and paying their owners.

4. The Emancipation Proclamation freed as many slaves as Lincoln believed he had the authority to free.

5. Lincoln supported the constitutional amendment that made slavery illegal.

People who believe the moral issue was not as important as Lincoln's desire to end the Civil War and preserve the Union use these points to support their position:

1. When Lincoln became president, his words assured slave owners that he had no plans to "interfere" with their slaves.

2. Lincoln supported a policy of colonizing blacks outside the United States.

3. The president overruled Union commanders who had freed slaves in captured Southern areas.

4. It took nearly two years of war before Lincoln issued the Preliminary Emancipation Proclamation.

5. The Emancipation Proclamation freed slaves only in the South.

Which side is correct? You have read about both sides of this issue. Either side might be right, or the truth may lie somewhere in between. Now consider both sides carefully. What do you think?

★ ★ ★ Time Line ★ ★ ★

Early 1600s Colonists use indentured servants

1619 Dutch traders bring African prisoners to the Virginia Colony and exchange them for goods

1600s Slave trade to colonies increases

1688 Pennsylvania Quakers protest the use of slaves

1701 Judge Samuel Sewall publishes his antislavery views

1776 Thomas Jefferson proposes to colonize blacks

1781 American colonies defeat Great Britain

1787 U.S. Constitution is created; slavery remains legal

late 1700s New England and Middle Atlantic states outlaw slavery

1793 Eli Whitney invents the cotton gin, creating an increased demand for slaves

1808 Congress makes it illegal to import slaves, but the practice continues

1831 Nat Turner leads a slave revolt in Virginia

Abolitionist William Lloyd Garrison founds *The Liberator*

1850 Congress passes the Fugitive Slave Act

1852 *Uncle Tom's Cabin*, by New England

abolitionist Harriet Beecher Stowe, is published

1850s Republican party is formed to help prevent the spread of slavery

The Underground Railroad helps slaves escape to the North

1857 U.S. Supreme Court rules against Dred Scott, a slave who had sued for his freedom

1859 John Brown raids a federal arsenal at Harpers Ferry to start a slave uprising; he is captured and hanged

1860 Republican Abraham Lincoln is elected president

South Carolina secedes

1861 **February** Confederate States of America is formed

April Confederate forces fire on Fort Sumter; the Civil War begins

December Lincoln proposes a colonization plan

1862 **March** Lincoln proposes a gradual emancipation plan

Spring Lincoln develops the Emancipation Proclamation

July Lincoln shares his plan with his cabinet; he decides to wait for another victory before announcing it

September Union wins at Antietam

September 22 Lincoln issues Preliminary Emancipation Proclamation

1863 **January 1** Lincoln signs the Emancipation Proclamation into law

December Constitutional amendment to free all slaves is introduced in Congress; it fails

1865 **April** Lee surrenders to Grant; the North wins the war

Lincoln is assassinated by John Wilkes Booth

December Thirteenth Amendment, making slavery illegal, is passed

1868 Fourteenth Amendment, providing equal rights to blacks, is passed

1870 Fifteenth Amendment, giving black male citizens the right to vote, is passed

★ ★ ★ Glossary ★ ★ ★

abolitionist—a person who wanted an immediate end to slavery

amendment—a change in the law, especially a change in the U.S. Constitution

blockade—the closing off of an area so that it cannot receive materials and supplies

border states—slaveholding states loyal to the Union: Missouri, Kentucky, Maryland, and Delaware, at the beginning of the war, and West Virginia in 1863

colonists—people who settle a distant land but are still subject to the parent country

Confederates—supporters of the Confederate States of America; also called rebels

Confederate States of America—the group of eleven Southern states that withdrew from the United States in 1860 and 1861. These states were Alabama, Arkansas, Florida, Georgia, Louisiana, Mississippi, North Carolina, South Carolina, Tennessee, Texas, and Virginia.

conscription—the government's selection of people for a required period of military service; draft

earthwork—a trench with a wooden framework and dirt in front

emancipate—to free

Emancipation Proclamation—President Lincoln's order, issued January 1, 1863, freeing slaves in Confederate states

enlist—to join the armed forces voluntarily

federal—referring to the United States government

inauguration—the ceremony in which a president takes the oath of office

indentured servant—a person who worked as a servant for a given period of time

moderates—in the Civil War period, people who opposed the spread of slavery

plantation—large farm in the South that used slaves as laborers

prejudice—hatred or unfair treatment of a particular group, such as members of a race or religion

rebels—soldiers fighting for the Confederate States of America

regiment—the basic army unit at the time of the Civil War; made up of approximately 1,000 men

tariff—a charge or tax that a government places on goods coming into a country

Union—referring to the United States and to the North during the Civil War

★ ★ ★ Appendix: ★ ★ ★
The Emancipation Proclamation

By the President of the United States of America
A Proclamation.

Whereas, on the twenty-second day of September, in the year of our Lord one thousand eight hundred and sixty-two, a proclamation was issued by the President of the United States, containing, among other things, the following, to wit:

"That on the first day of January, in the year of our Lord one thousand eight hundred and sixty-three, all persons held as slaves within any State or designated part of a State, the people whereof shall then be in rebellion against the United States, shall be then, thenceforward, and forever free; and the Executive Government of the United States, including the military and naval authority thereof, will recognize and maintain the freedom of such persons, and will do no act or acts to repress such persons, or any of them, in any efforts they may make for their actual freedom.

"That the Executive will, on the first day of January aforesaid, by proclamation, designate the States and parts of States, if any, in which the people thereof, respectively, shall then be in rebellion against the United States; and the fact that any State, or the people thereof, shall on that day be, in good faith, represented in the Congress of the United States by members chosen thereto at elections wherein a majority of the qualified voters of such State shall have participated, shall, in the absence of strong countervailing testimony, be deemed conclusive evidence that such State, and the people thereof, are not then in rebellion against the United States."

Now, therefore, I, Abraham Lincoln, President of the United States, by virtue of the power in me vested as Commander-in-Chief, of the Army and Navy of the United States in time of actual armed rebellion against the authority and government of the United States, and as a fit and necessary war measure for suppressing said rebellion, do, on this first day of January, in the year of our Lord one thousand eight hundred and sixty-three, and in accordance with my purpose so to do publicly proclaimed for the full period of one hundred days, from the day first above mentioned, order and designate as the States and parts of States wherein the people thereof respectively, are this day in rebellion against the United States, the following, to wit:

Arkansas, Texas, Louisiana, (except the Parishes of St. Bernard, Plaquemines, Jefferson, St. John, St. Charles, St. James Ascension, Assumption, Terrebonne, Lafourche, St. Mary, St. Martin, and Orleans, including the City of New-Orleans) Mississippi, Alabama, Florida, Georgia, South Carolina, North Carolina, and Virginia, (except the forty-eight counties designated as West Virginia, and also the counties of Berkley, Accomac, Northampton, Elizabeth City, York, Princess Ann, and Norfolk, including the cities of Norfolk and Portsmouth, and which excepted parts are, for the present, left precisely as if this proclamation were not issued.

And by virtue of the power, and for the purpose aforesaid, I do order and declare that all persons held as slaves within said designated States, and parts of States, are, and henceforward shall be, free; and that the Executive government of the United States, including the military and naval authorities thereof, will recognize and maintain the freedom of said persons.

And I hereby enjoin upon the people so declared to be free to abstain from all violence, unless in necessary self-defence; and I recommend to them that, in all cases when allowed, they labor faithfully for reasonable wages.

And I further declare and make known, that such persons of suitable condition, will be received into the armed service of the United States to garrison forts, positions, stations, and other places, and to man vessels of all sorts in said service.

And upon this act, sincerely believed to be an act of justice, warranted by the Constitution, upon military necessity, I invoke the considerate judgment of mankind, and the gracious favor of Almighty God.

In witness whereof, I have hereunto set my hand and caused the seal of the United States to be affixed.

Done at the city of Washington, this first day of January, in the year of our Lord one thousand eight hundred and sixty three, and of the Independence of the United States of America the eighty-seventh.

By the President: Abraham Lincoln

William H. Seward, Secretary of State.

★   For Further Reading   ★

If you would like to know more about slavery and the Civil War, here are some articles and books that were helpful in writing *The Emancipation Proclamation: Why Lincoln Really Freed the Slaves.*

ARTICLES

Adler, Jerry. "Revisiting the Civil War." *Newsweek* (October 8, 1990).

Durham, Michael S. "The Word Is Slaves: A Trip into Black History." *American Heritage* (April 1992).

Morgenthau, Tom. "Slavery: How It Built the New World." *Newsweek* (Fall-Winter 1991).

BOOKS

Catton, Bruce. *The American Heritage Picture History of the Civil War.* New York: American Heritage, 1982.

Evitts, William J. *Captive Bodies, Free Spirits.* New York: Julian Messner, 1985.

Franklin, John Hope. *From Slavery to Freedom: A History of Negro Americans.* New York: Alfred A. Knopf, 1988.

Freedman, Russell. *Lincoln: An Autobiography.* New York: Scholastic, 1987.

Jordan, Robert Paul. *The Civil War.* Washington, D.C.: National Geographic, 1969.

McPherson, James M. *Battle Cry of Freedom.* New York: Oxford University Press, 1988.

Meltzer, Milton. *Voices from the Civil War.* New York: Crowell, 1989.

Myers, Walter Dean. *Now Is Your Time: The African-American Struggle for Freedom.* New York: HarperCollins, 1991.

Oates, Stephen B. *With Malice Toward None: The Life of Abraham Lincoln.* New York: Harper & Row, 1977.

Ray, Delia. *Behind the Blue and Gray.* New York: Penguin, 1991.

Ray, Delia. *A Nation Torn.* New York: Dutton, 1990.

Robertson, James I., Jr. *Civil War!* New York: Alfred A. Knopf, 1992.

★ ★ ★ ★ Index ★ ★ ★ ★

★ ★ About the Author ★ ★

Robert Young has been fascinated with the past ever since he walked through the house in which George Washington once lived. Besides writing books that help bring history alive, Robert job-shares a teaching position and visits schools to speak about writing. The author of ten books for children and teachers, Robert lives in Eugene, Oregon, with his wife, Sara, and their son, Tyler.

WITHDRAWN